11/02

0x 1/13

CR

D0688495

MATTHEW HENSON

DISCOVER THE LIFE OF AN AMERICAN LEGEND

David and Patricia Armentrout

Rourke

Publishing LLC
Vero Beach, Florida 32964

www.rourkepublishing.com

PHOTO CREDITS: ©Library of Congress Cover, pages 4, 7, 8, 17, 18, 21; © Corel Corporation Title page, pages12, 15; © NOAA page 10

Cover: *Arctic explorer Matthew Henson*

Title page : *Strong dogs pull Arctic sledges.*

Editor: Frank Sloan

Cover design by Nicola Stratford

Library of Congress Cataloging-in-Publication Data

Armentrout, David, 1962-
  Matthew Henson / David and Patricia Armentrout.
      v. cm. — (Discover the life of an American legend)
Includes bibliographical references and index.
Contents: Explorer — Matthew Henson — A better life - Nicaragua — First Arctic Expedition — Greenland —
Survival in the Arctic — One more trip — The North Pole — Dates to remember.
  ISBN 1-58952-658-9
  1. Henson, Matthew Alexander, 1866-1955—Juvenile literature. 2.
African-American explorers—Biography—Juvenile literature. 3. North
Pole—Discovery and exploration—Juvenile literature. [1. Henson, Matthew Alexander, 1866-1955. 2.
Explorers. 3.African-Americans—Biography. 4. North Pole--Discovery and exploration.] I. Armentrout,
Patricia, 1960- II. Title. III. Series.
  G635.H4A76 2003
  919.8—dc21

                                                        2003002210

Printed in the USA

CG/CG

Table of Contents

Explorer

People love to explore and discover new places. Some of our greatest heroes are those who have taken great risks to explore unfamiliar places. Matthew Henson is one such explorer. In the late 1800s and early 1900s Matthew Henson and Robert Peary explored one of the coldest regions on Earth. They would also attempt to be the first humans to reach the North Pole.

Matthew Henson shows President Dwight D. Eisenhower his 1909 exploration route.

Matthew Henson

Matthew Alexander Henson was born August 8, 1866 in Maryland. The Civil War had just ended. Slavery would never again be legal in the United States, but African Americans still did not enjoy equal rights. As an African American, Matthew would face **racism** and unfair treatment for much of his life.

Matthew held numerous jobs before and after his Arctic expeditions.

Quadrant.

1. Buoy   2. Cleat   3. Bulls eye   4. Reflecting Circle.   5. Large Cleat   6. Caispaise   7. Chain Cable.

Sextant.

1. Bowsprit.   6. Fore top gallant mast 11. Fore royal yard   16. Main yard   21. Mizen top mast   26. Mizen top gall? yard
2. Jib boom   7. Fore royal mast   12. Main mast   17. Main top sail yard 22. Mizen top gall? mast 27. Mizen royal yard.
3. Sprit sail yard   8. Fore yard   13. Main top mast   18. Main top galland yard 23. Mizen royal mast   28. Gaff.
4. Fore Mast.   9. Fore top sail yard   14. Main top galland mast 19. Main royal yard   24. Cross jack yard   29. Stem
5. Fore top mast   10. Fore top gallant yard 15. Main royal mast   20. Mizen mast   25. Mizen top yard   30. Stern

1. ...pe 2. Shroud laid rope 3. Hawser laid ro...

...rling spoke 2. Anchor 3. An Euphroe 4. Fid

1. Dead eye 2. Top block   3. Tail block
4. Cat block 5. Three fold block

1. Spun yarn winch. 2. Marling spike 3...

Published by the AMERICAN SUNDAY SCHOOL UNION, N? 146 Chesnut St. Philadelphia.

A Better Life

Matthew's mother died when he was only two years old. His father remarried, but his new wife treated Matthew badly. When his father died a few years later, Matthew left home looking for a better life. He was 11 years old.

Matthew found a job as a cabin boy on a ship. The ship sailed to distant ports in China, Japan, North Africa, and Russia. He learned to be a sailor.

Matthew learned to use the many instruments needed on board sailing vessels.

Nicaragua

Matthew Henson and Robert Peary met in 1887. Peary was a U.S. Navy engineer. He had been instructed to find the best place to dig a canal across Nicaragua. The canal would connect the Atlantic and Pacific oceans and would save ships weeks of travel time. Peary hired Henson to be his personal assistant for the **expedition**.

Robert Peary around the time of his Nicaraguan expedition

First Arctic Expedition

Soon after the Nicaraguan expedition, Peary began planning his second expedition to the **Arctic** regions of Greenland, a mostly unexplored piece of land on top of the world. He asked Henson to be part of his team. Among the team members was Frederick Cook. Cook later claimed to have beaten Peary and Henson to the North Pole on his own Arctic expedition. Most historians believe his claim to be false.

Arctic explorers endure a cold, harsh environment.

Greenland

In 1891, Peary's team traveled by ship as far north as they could. Packed on board were supplies to last more than two years. After a long trip through dangerous seas, the team went ashore in Greenland. Henson's first job was to build a shelter for the team to spend the winter. Local **Inuit** natives taught Henson and the others how to survive in the frigid Arctic. Henson learned to build **igloos** and to drive dog **sledges**.

Building an igloo

Survival in the Arctic

In the spring of 1892 the expedition set off to cross Greenland. The team struggled against bitter cold and icy winds. At one point Henson was forced to turn back. Even though he wore heavy fur boots, his heel had become **frostbitten**. Henson's trip was over, but he would have other opportunities to explore the Arctic. Henson and Peary would travel to the Arctic six more times, each time gaining valuable experience.

Peary, shown here, wearing the traditional warm clothing of the Inuit

One More Trip

Peary was determined to reach the North Pole. He knew Matthew Henson could help him get there. In the summer of 1908, they set off one more time, bound for the Arctic. Peary asked Inuit natives to be part of the expedition. Hundreds of dogs were brought on board the ship. The dogs would pull the heavy sledges over the snow and ice. The team spent the winter months camped in northern Canada preparing for the journey over the frozen Arctic Ocean.

North Pole expedition base camp under construction

The North Pole

In late February, the team drove their dog sledges out over the frozen sea. As supplies ran low, Peary ordered some of the team members to return to camp. Finally, only Peary, Henson, and four Inuit men were left.

On April 6, 1909, the party reached the North Pole. Robert Peary became famous for his expedition. Matthew Henson wrote a book about his adventures titled *A Negro Explorer at the North Pole.* Matthew Henson died in 1955.

Matthew Henson holding a photograph of Robert Peary

Dates to Remember

1866	Matthew Alexander Henson is born on August 8 in Charles County, Maryland
1868	Matthew's mother dies
1877	Leaves home to search for a better life
1878	Hired as a cabin boy on an ocean-going vessel
1887	Peary hires Henson for an expedition to Nicaragua
1891	Henson's first expedition to Greenland
1908	Final North Pole expedition
1909	Robert Peary, Matthew Henson, and four Inuit men reach the North Pole on April 6
1955	Matthew Henson dies in New York City

Glossary

Arctic (ARK tik) — the frozen area that surrounds the North Pole

expedition (ek spuh DISH uhn) — a long journey for a special purpose such as exploring

frostbitten (FRAWST bit in) — when a body part becomes frozen and damaged due to cold temperatures

igloos (IG looz) — dome-shaped shelters built of ice, snow, earth, wood, or stone

Inuit (IN oo it) — a group of people from the Arctic, sometimes called Eskimos

racism (RAY sis um) — the belief that one race is superior, or better, than another

sledges (SLEDJ ez) — strong, heavy sleds pulled by dogs

Index

Further Reading

Gaines, Ann Graham. *Matthew Henson and the North Pole Expedition*. Childs World, 2001.
Henson, Matthew. *A Negro Explorer at the North Pole*. Invisible Cities Press, 2001.
Litwin, Laura Baskes. *Co-Discoverer of the North Pole*. Enslow Publishers, Inc., 2001.

Websites To Visit

www.northpole1909.com/
www.arctic.noaa.gov/gallery.html
www.unmuseum.org/henson.htm

About The Authors

David and Patricia Armentrout have written many nonfiction books for young readers. They specialize in science and social studies topics. They have had several books published for primary school reading. The Armentrouts live in Cincinnati, Ohio, with their two children.